Kingdomkids

Kashlly Kingdom Kids

www.Thejourneytofindgod.com

Scan for more books by
Ashley Lunnon

15 Bedtime Prayers: For Kidz , 2023

Kingdom Kids
Rocky Mount NC
www.Thejourneytofindgod.com

This Book Belongs To:

_____

WELCOME

This book is lovingly crafted to bring comfort, peace, and love to the nighttime routine of young hearts and minds. Bedtime prayers have a special place in a child's life, offering them a moment of tranquility, connection, and reflection before they drift off to sleep.

Within the pages of this book, you will find a collection of heartfelt prayers designed to nurture a sense of gratitude, safety, and love. Each prayer is a gentle invitation to embrace the wonders of the day, seek blessings for loved ones, and find solace in the embrace of a peaceful night's rest.

As you embark on this enchanting journey, let the soothing words and calming rhythms guide you into a world of dreams. Whether you are seeking comfort, expressing thanks, or simply enjoying a moment of quiet reflection, these prayers are here to accompany you on your bedtime adventures.

May this book become a cherished companion, fostering a deep connection with God, and nurturing a sense of peace and serenity within the hearts of our little ones. Together, let us embark on a journey of love, gratitude, and tranquility as we enter the realm of dreams.

May this book become a cherished tradition, a whispered companion, and a source of comfort for countless nights to come.

With love and blessings,
Ashley Lunnon

EXPRESSING GRATITUDE TO GOD FOR THE DAY

"Dear God,

As I lay in my bed, ready to rest my weary head,
I close my eyes and bow my little prayerful heart.
Thank You, dear God, for this day that's come to an end,
For the love and blessings You always send.

Thank You for the sun that shone so bright,
For the birds that sang with all their might.
Thank You for the laughter, the games, and play,
For the moments that made me smile today.

Thank You for the food that filled my plate,
For the water I drank and the moments we ate.
Thank You for my family, loving and true,
For their warm hugs and "I love you."

Thank You for my friends, so kind and dear,
For the joy they bring, always near.
Thank You for the teachers who guide my way,
For the knowledge and wisdom they share each day.

Thank You for the stars that twinkle above,
For the moon's gentle glow and the gift of love.
Thank You for keeping me safe and secure,
For watching over me, of that I am sure.

As I close my eyes and drift to sleep,
Please bless and protect me through the night so deep.
Grant me peaceful dreams till the morning light,
And wake me up refreshed and shining bright.

Thank You, dear God, for everything You do,
For being with me, for loving me too.
In Your hands, I place my worries and cares,
Knowing that You are always there.

With grateful hearts, we say goodnight,
Resting in Your loving and guiding light.

Amen.

May this bedtime prayer bring comfort, gratitude, and a sense of peace
to children as they prepare to sleep.

EXPRESSING GRATITUDE AND LOVE FOR YOUR PARENTS

Heavenly Father,

As I lay down to rest, I lift up a prayer,
To thank You for the parents who love and care.
For Mom and Dad, who are always there,
Guiding and supporting with tender love to share.

Thank You for the hugs they give so tight,
For wiping away my tears and bringing back the light.
Thank You for the laughter, the stories they tell,
For the bedtime rituals that make my heart swell.

Bless Mom and Dad with health and happiness,
Fill their hearts with love and peace.
Grant them strength when they're feeling tired,
And patience when my antics might have them wired.

Thank You for the lessons they patiently teach,
For the words of wisdom they softly preach.
Help me show gratitude and kindness each day,
To let them know their love won't fade away.

In their arms, I find solace and security,
Their love surrounds me with pure sincerity.
Please watch over them with Your guiding light,
And bless them with dreams that are peaceful and bright.

Thank You, dear God, for my parents so dear,
For their selfless love that is always near.
I am grateful for their nurturing embrace,
And the warmth they bring to this sacred space.

In Your name, I pray, with a grateful heart,
As I close my eyes and prepare to depart,
Into the realm of dreams and peaceful sleep,
Bless Mom and Dad, their love I'll always keep.

Amen.

May this prayer serve as a heartfelt expression of love and gratitude for parents,
fostering a deeper appreciation and connection within the family.

I HAD A TOUGH DAY

Dear God,

As I lay here in my bed, weary and worn,
I come to You tonight, feeling forlorn.
Today was tough, with challenges in my way,
But I know You are with me, come what may.

When things were hard and I felt alone,
You were there, my strength and my comfort zone.
Thank You for listening when I felt small,
For catching my tears when they started to fall.

In times of struggle, You're my guiding light,
Helping me find courage and the will to fight.
Thank You for the lessons learned through the day,
For the growth that happens when things don't go my way.

Please bring me peace as I close my eyes,
Release my worries and quiet my cries.
Wrap me in Your love, so warm and true,
And mend my spirit with Your gentle dew.

Grant me restful sleep, a time to restore,
So I wake up tomorrow, ready for more.
Help me face each challenge with strength and grace,
Knowing Your presence is always in this space.

Thank You, dear God, for being by my side,
In the highs and lows, You are my guide.
With Your love and light, I'll find my way,
Even on tough days, I'll trust and pray.

Amen.

May this prayer bring comfort, solace, and renewed strength to children as
they reflect on a tough day and find reassurance in God's presence.

SIBLINGS

Dear God,

As I prepare for sleep, I kneel down to pray,
Thank You for the sibling with whom I play.
You've blessed me with a sister/brother so dear,
A companion for life, forever near.

Thank You for the laughter we share each day,
For the adventures we embark on in our own special way.
Through ups and downs, we stand side by side,
In joy and comfort, our bond cannot hide.

Thank You for the moments we spend together,
Creating memories that will last forever.
For the games we play and the secrets we share,
For the love and support that shows You care.

Bless my sister/brother with Your grace and light,
Guide them on their journey, both day and night.
May they find happiness in all they pursue,
And know that Your love for them is true.

Help us cherish our sibling bond so strong,
Through disagreements and when things go wrong.
Teach us patience, forgiveness, and compassion,
In our relationship, may we find endless passion.

Thank You, dear God, for my sibling's love,
A gift from You, shining from above.
May our connection grow deeper and strong,
A bond that will endure, forever long.

Amen.

May this prayer be a heartfelt expression of gratitude for the
precious gift of siblings and a reminder of the love and support
they bring into our lives.

SEEKING GUIDANCE AND BLESSINGS FOR THE DAY AHEAD

"Dear Heavenly Father,

As the day comes to a close and darkness falls,
I come before You, Lord, on bended knees, I call.
Grant me a peaceful rest, as I lay down to sleep,
And hear my prayer, dear God, my soul to keep.

Tomorrow lies ahead, a new day to embrace,
With challenges and blessings I will surely face.
Guide my footsteps, Lord, as I navigate each choice,
Fill my heart with wisdom, let Your voice be my voice.

Grant me clarity to see the right path to pursue,
Strength to overcome obstacles, both old and new.
Help me be kind and compassionate to all I meet,
To spread Your love and light, making their lives sweet.

Give me courage to face challenges with resolve,
To never give up, knowing in You I can evolve.
Open my eyes to opportunities that come my way,
And help me make the most of each moment, I pray.

Grant me patience and understanding, dear God,
To navigate relationships with grace, never flawed.
May my words and actions bring joy and cheer,
And may I be a source of comfort to those who are near.

In all that I do, may Your guidance be clear,
I trust in Your plan, knowing You are always near.
Thank You for being my compass, my guiding star,
I surrender to Your will, knowing You'll never be far.

As I close my eyes and drift into the night,
I place my trust in You, my Guiding Light.
Bless me with a restful sleep and a hopeful heart,
As I awaken tomorrow, ready for a brand new start.

Amen.

May this prayer bring comfort, reassurance, and a sense of guidance to children as
they seek God's wisdom and blessings for the day ahead.

MY UNIQUENESS

Dear Heavenly Father,

In this quiet moment, as I prepare to rest,
I come before You, grateful and blessed.
Thank You for creating me in a special way,
Unique and precious, with purpose every day.

I thank You for my quirks and the traits I possess,
For the talents and abilities that make me different, no less.
You've given me a voice to sing and words to express,
A heart that feels deeply, a spirit I am here to impress.

Thank You for the strengths that set me apart,
For the passions that ignite a fire within my heart.
Help me embrace the person I'm meant to be,
And use my gifts to serve You faithfully.

When doubts arise, and I question who I am,
Remind me, dear God, that You have a perfect plan.
You've molded me with care, each detail unique,
A masterpiece in progress, ever evolving and sleek.

Thank You for the ways I see the world around,
For the perspective and insight that I have found.
Bless me with confidence, embracing my true worth,
Knowing that my uniqueness is a treasure from birth.

May I celebrate diversity in others I meet,
Seeing the beauty in every person I greet.
Grant me the wisdom to appreciate and understand,
That we are all wonderfully made by Your loving hand.

Thank You, dear God, for the gift of being me,
For the love and acceptance You continuously decree.
As I close my eyes, I rest in Your loving embrace,
Thankful for my uniqueness, full of Your grace.

Amen."

May this prayer remind children to appreciate their individuality and the special
qualities that make them who they are, knowing that they are fearfully and
wonderfully made by God.

SEEKING GOD'S PROTECTION:

Heavenly Father,

As the day draws to a close and the night unfolds,
I come before You, Lord, with a heart that longs to be consoled.
I ask for Your loving presence to surround me now,
And for Your divine protection, I humbly bow.

Watch over me, dear God, as I lay down to sleep,
Keep me safe within Your embrace, so tender and deep.
Protect me from any harm, seen and unseen,
Guide me through the darkness, make my path serene.

Shield me from fear that may try to take hold,
Fill my heart with courage, bold and bold.
Wrap me in Your arms, a shield strong and true,
Let Your love be my armor, seeing me through.

Guard my dreams, dear Lord, as I rest my weary mind,
Bring peaceful visions, tranquility I find.
Keep away the nightmares, banish them afar,
Replace them with dreams that sparkle like a stars.

Protect my home, my family, and all dear to me,
Watch over us with Your grace, eternally.
Surround us with Your angels, a heavenly host,
Defend us from danger, like a protective coast.

In Your care, I find solace and peace,
Knowing that Your love for me will never cease.
Thank You for the assurance of Your steadfast love,
And for the protection that comes from above.

As I surrender to sleep, I trust in Your might,
Knowing that You are with me, both day and night.
Thank You, dear God, for the safety You impart,
I rest in Your loving hands, for You are my guard.

Amen."

May this prayer provide comfort, reassurance, and a deep sense of God's
protection for children as they lay down to sleep, knowing that they are under
His watchful care.

SEEKING WISDOM

Dear Heavenly Father,

As I prepare for sleep, I come to You in prayer,
Seeking Your divine wisdom, so loving and fair.
Grant me, dear Lord, a mind open and clear,
Fill it with knowledge and wisdom, drawing near.

I ask for wisdom to make choices that are right,
To discern between darkness and the shining light.
Guide me in each decision, big and small,
Grant me understanding, so I won't stumble or fall.

Help me see the world with compassionate eyes,
To empathize with others, and hear their heartfelt cries.
Grant me the wisdom to treat all with respect,
To value differences and love without neglect.

Teach me to be patient, to listen and learn,
To seek knowledge and wisdom at every turn.
May Your truth be my compass, leading the way,
As I navigate life's challenges, day by day.

Grant me wisdom in my words, to speak with care,
To bring comfort and encouragement, showing I'm aware.
Help me use my voice for kindness and truth,
To make a positive impact, for the benefit of youth.

In all my pursuits, let wisdom be my guide,
To make choices that reflect Your love deep inside.
Bless me with discernment, a heart that is wise,
To see the beauty in the world through Your eyes.

Thank You, dear God, for hearing my prayer,
For the wisdom You provide, beyond compare.
As I close my eyes and surrender to sleep's embrace,
Grant me wisdom for tomorrow, through Your grace.

Amen."

May this prayer serve as a heartfelt request for wisdom,
guiding children to seek knowledge, make wise choices, and
navigate the world with understanding and compassion.

ASKING GOD TO WATCH OVER AND BLESS HOMELESS PEOPLE

Heavenly Father,

In this moment of quiet reflection, I turn to You,
With a prayer in my heart for those without a home, so few.
Please hear my plea, dear Lord, as I bow my head,
Wrap Your arms around the homeless, who are in need.

Watch over them, dear God, in their time of despair,
Provide shelter from the elements, show them You care.
Protect them from danger and keep them safe at night,
Comfort them with Your presence, shining so bright.

In the cold and loneliness they may face,
Send warmth to their hearts, with Your endless grace.
Provide nourishment for their bodies and souls,
Sustain them through hardship, filling their empty bowls.

Help us, dear God, to see their worth and their worthiness,
To extend our hands in kindness and selflessness.
Guide us to be instruments of Your love and care,
To offer compassion and support, showing we are aware.

May we open our hearts to their plight and their pain,
To ease their burdens, so they know they're not in vain.
Give us the courage to break down barriers and walls,
And to advocate for justice, until every voice calls.

Dear Lord, bless the homeless with hope and resilience,
Strengthen their spirits in the face of their existence.
Help us create a world where no one is left behind,
Where shelter, compassion, and love they can find.

In Your name, I pray, with a heart that is true,
As I close my eyes and entrust them to You.
May Your love shine upon them, a beacon so bright,
Guiding them to a home, filled with love and light.

Amen."

May this prayer remind children to recognize and care for those
who are homeless, and may it inspire compassion, empathy, and
action towards creating a more just and inclusive society.

ASKING GOD FOR FORGIVENESS

Dear Heavenly Father,

I come before You with a humble heart,
Seeking Your forgiveness, knowing we're not apart.
I ask for Your mercy and grace so divine,
For the mistakes I've made, please help me realign.

Forgive me, dear God, for the times I've gone astray,
For the hurtful words I've spoken or actions on display.
I know I'm not perfect, I stumble and fall,
But with Your forgiveness, I can rise above it all.

Please cleanse my heart from any wrongdoing,
Wash away my sins, restore the song I should sing.
I ask for Your loving hand to guide me anew,
To live a life that's pleasing and honorable to You.

Help me learn from my mistakes, dear Lord,
To grow in wisdom and understanding, as You've implored.
Grant me strength to resist temptation's snare,
And to live a life that shows how much I care.

Thank You for Your boundless love and grace,
For forgiving me, putting my faults in their rightful place.
Help me extend that forgiveness to others, too,
Showing them Your mercy in all that I do.

I am grateful for Your forgiveness, dear God,
For the chance to start fresh, as on this path I trod.
With a contrite heart, I seek Your embrace,
Knowing that Your forgiveness is a boundless space.

In Your loving arms, I find solace and peace,
Knowing that Your forgiveness will never cease.
Thank You for hearing my prayer, so sincere,
As I seek Your forgiveness, drawing You near.

Amen."

May this prayer help children seek God's forgiveness with a sincere heart,
knowing that His love and mercy are always available to guide them on
their journey of growth and redemption.

SCHOOL ENDEAVORS

Heavenly Father,

As I bow my head and come to You in prayer,
I ask for Your guidance and assistance, so loving and fair.
Please help me in my studies as I go to school each day,
Grant me wisdom, understanding, and strength along the way.

I pray for clarity of mind, to grasp new concepts with ease,
Give me a hunger for knowledge, a passion that never ceases.
Grant me the ability to focus and concentrate,
To absorb information and to participate.

Bless my teachers, who work tirelessly each day,
Give them patience, wisdom, and kind words to say.
May they inspire me to learn, to discover and explore,
To grow in knowledge, unlocking each door.

Help me to be organized, with diligence and care,
To manage my time wisely, with tasks I need to bear.
Grant me the discipline to complete assignments on time,
To study and prepare, so my efforts will shine.

When challenges arise, and I feel overwhelmed,
Remind me of Your presence, that I am not alone in this realm.
Fill my heart with confidence, banish doubts and fear,
Knowing that with You by my side, success is near.

Grant me good friendships, with classmates true and kind,
May we support and encourage each other, a bond that's hard to find.
Help us to create a positive learning environment,
Where respect, compassion, and acceptance are inherent.

Thank You, dear God, for the opportunity to learn and grow,
For the gift of education, a pathway we can sow.
May Your light guide me through each lesson and test,
And may I use my knowledge to serve and do my best.

In Your hands, I place my studies, trusting in Your care,
Knowing that with Your help, I will succeed.
Thank You for hearing my prayer, so sincere,
As I seek Your assistance in school, drawing You near.

Amen.

May this prayer inspire children to seek God's help and guidance in
their academic pursuits, fostering a love for learning and a mindset
of diligence and perseverance.

WORLD PEACE

Dear Heavenly Father,

In a world filled with turmoil and strife,
I come before You, seeking peace in this life.
I pray for unity, understanding, and love,
To bring harmony to this world, like a gentle dove.

Please, dear God, heal the wounds of war,
Bring an end to conflicts that leave hearts sore.
Guide leaders and nations with wisdom and grace,
To work together for peace, in every place.

Help us embrace our differences, big and small,
To celebrate diversity and break down each wall.
May kindness and empathy fill every heart,
And may peace and compassion be our world's work of art.

Bring peace to those living in fear and despair,
Protect the innocent, show them You care.
Comfort those affected by violence and strife,
And lead us all towards a harmonious life.

Instill in us, dear Lord, a desire to understand,
To seek common ground, holding each other's hand.
Let us sow seeds of peace in all that we do,
Creating a world where peace and love shine through.

May we be peacemakers, spreading kindness and light,
Standing up for justice, with all of our might.
Grant us the courage to make a difference, however small,
And help us create a world where peace reigns over all.

Thank You, dear God, for hearing our plea,
For Your infinite love that sets our hearts free.
May Your peace permeate every corner of this Earth,
Bringing hope, healing, and a renewed sense of worth.

Amen."

May this prayer inspire children to seek peace, practice kindness,
and work towards creating a more peaceful and harmonious world,
where love and compassion prevail over conflict and division.

HEALTH AND SAFETY

Heavenly Father,

In this moment of prayer, I turn to You,
Seeking Your loving care, so gentle and true.
I ask for Your blessings of health and safety,
For me, my family, and all humanity.

Please watch over us with Your guiding hand,
Protect us in ways only You understand.
Keep us safe from harm, both day and night,
Surround us with Your love, shining so bright.

Grant us good health, body, mind, and soul,
May Your healing power make us whole.
Guard us against illnesses, seen and unseen,
Strengthen our immune systems, keep them keen.

Protect us from accidents, mishaps, and strife,
Keep us safe in every step of our life.
Guide us away from dangers, big and small,
And shield us from harm's way, once and for all.

Dear God, be our rock and our fortress strong,
Defend us from all that could go wrong.
Cover us with Your wings, a shelter so secure,
Where we find solace and feel reassured.

For those who are sick, I lift up my prayer,
Send them comfort, relief, and tender care.
Bring healing to their bodies, gentle and swift,
Restore their health, with Your loving gift.

Thank You, dear God, for Your watchful eye,
For the assurance that You're always nearby.
May Your love and protection be our guiding light,
Keeping us safe and healthy, day and night.

Amen."

May this prayer bring comfort, assurance, and a sense of God's protection and
healing for children, their families, and all those in need of health and safety.

PERSONAL DREAMS AND GOALS

Dear Heavenly Father,

I come before You in humble prayer,
Seeking Your guidance, knowing You're always there.
I bring to You my dreams, my goals so dear,
Asking for Your help, Your presence so near.

Lord, You know the desires within my heart,
The dreams I hold, where my passions start.
Grant me the courage to pursue them with zeal,
To work hard, to strive, and to never yield.

Please bless my endeavors, dear God above,
Fill me with wisdom, grace, and unfailing love.
Guide me along the path I'm meant to tread,
Direct my steps, where my dreams are led.

In moments of doubt, when challenges arise,
Remind me of Your promise, the strength in Your eyes.
Help me trust in Your plan, when mine seems unclear,
Knowing that You hold my dreams ever near.

Grant me patience as I strive for my goals,
Teach me to learn from failures and to reach new roles.
Keep my focus steady, my spirit strong,
As I journey towards where I truly belong.

Provide me with mentors, wise and true,
To guide and inspire, helping my dreams come into view.
Surround me with loved ones, supportive and kind,
Who uplift my spirit and believe in what I'm designed.

May my dreams align with Your divine will,
And may my efforts be driven by love, not for self-will.
Help me use my talents to serve and make a change,
To bring hope, joy, and blessings within my range.

Thank You, dear God, for the dreams within my soul,
For the gifts You've bestowed, making me whole.
With Your help, I know I can reach for the sky,
And make a difference, as dreams soar high.

In Your name, I pray, with a heart that's true,
Trusting Your guidance, as my dreams I pursue.
Thank You for hearing my prayer, so sincere,
As I seek Your help in achieving my dreams, drawing You near.

Amen.

May this prayer uplift and encourage children as they seek God's help in pursuing
their personal dreams and goals, reminding them that with His guidance and
support, they can fulfill their potential and make a positive impact in the world.